ALCOHOLIC WINE AND THE CHRISTIAN

Dennis H. Helton

Alcoholic Wine and the Christian
Copyright © 2021 by Dennis Helton
All Rights Reserved
Printed in the United States of America
May 2021

ISBN: 978-1-7365344-0-3

All Scripture quotes are from the King James Bible

No part of this work may be reproduced without the expressed consent of the publisher, except for brief quotes, whether by electronic, photocopying, recording, or information storage and retrieval systems.

Address All Inquiries To:
THE OLD PATHS PUBLICATIONS, Inc.
142 Gold Flume Way
Cleveland, Georgia, U.S.A.

Web: www.theoldpathspublications.com
E-mail: TOP@theoldpathspublications.com

DEDICATION

PREFACE

The title of this book, *Alcoholic Wine and the Christian* may seem strange to some. However, it defines an issue that permeates Christianity today because the word, "wine," is found often in the preserved Words of the Bible. The word "wine" is a polysemic word. That is, (1) it has different meanings depending upon its context, (2) its definition and exegesis is derived from the many words underlying the translation from the original languages of Hebrew and Greek given by God, and (3) its cultural use.

Brother Helton's book, *Alcoholic Wine and the Christian,* is so needed in these last days because alcohol has become a scourge upon humanity, not in America only, but throughout the world. The scourge, which has accelerated iniquity worldwide, has occurred for several reasons. (1) overt sin (drunkenness), (2) a misunderstanding of the Bible, (3) the corruption of the clear statements in Scripture by uneducated, misinformed preachers, teachers, missionaries, laymen, and authors (4) the pressures brought upon societies from the "so-called" SARS-CoV-2 pandemic, (5) humanistic culture that abounds because of *"the tradition of men, after the rudiments of the world and not after Christ."* (Colossians 2:8), (6) The false advertising of the liquor industry (e.g., alcohol is good for your heart and prevents cancer), (7) the self-indulgent culture of affluent nations, and (8) the promotion by the entertainment, TV, and social media industry.

God said to the nation Israel, after it had been blessed by God (just as America has been blessed by God, but her people do not recognize their benefactor) in Ezekiel 16:49: *Behold, this was the iniquity of thy sister Sodom, pride, fulness of bread, and abundance of idleness was in her and in her daughters, neither did she strengthen the hand of the poor and needy.* Note the 3 causes of iniquity: (1) pride, (2) fulness of bread (wealth), (3) idleness. Idleness has been brought on in this country partly by the government's indiscriminate payments to idle, lazy individuals.

Here are some statistics for you to ponder concerning alcoholism or alcohol abuse:

- Alcohol sales increased by 54% in the week ending 21 March 2020 due to stay-at-home orders.
- Alcohol-related deaths rose by 43% between 2006 and 2018.
- 86.4% of adults admit to drinking alcohol at least once in their lifetimes.
- 80% of college students consume alcohol.
- 15.1 million adults in the US aged 18 and older have an alcohol use disorder.
- Over 10% of kids in the US live with a parent that has alcohol issues.
- 33.1% of 15-year-olds report having had at least one drink so far in their lifetime.
- Drinking and driving accounts for over 30% of all driving deaths a year.
- More than 65 million Americans reported binge drinking within a month of being surveyed.

(from "35 Sobering Alcoholism Statistics and Facts for 2021 disturbmenot.co," http://disturbmenot.co/alcoholism-statistics/)

Social drinkers, who claim they are not causing harm because they are not involved in intemperate drinking and therefore are "OK" with God because they drink responsibly (moderately), need to be aware of their influence on (1) children, (2) "babes" in Christ, and (3) the "carnal" Christian.

God says: **1 Thessalonians 5:22** *"Abstain from all appearance of evil.* That is a command, not a choice.

Drinking Alcohol and everything associated with it is evil. Brother Helton has done an excellent job bringing out the precepts associated with the issue of alcohol.

H. D. Williams, M.D., Ph.D., President
The Old Paths Publications
142 Gold Flume Way,
Cleveland, GA 30528

TABLE OF CONTENTS

ALCOHOLIC WINE AND THE CHRISTIAN

Comments by Robert Sumner

The following is an edited review of Dr. Jaeggli's book *THE CHRISTIAN AND DRINKING: A BIBLICAL PERSPECTIVE ON MODERATION AND ABSTINENCE* by Randy Jaeggli; BJU Press, Greenville, SC by Robert Sumner, editor of the *Biblical Evangelist* newspaper, which was published in the July-August 2009 issue.

This is a new release in the "BJU-Press Biblical Discernment for Difficult Issues," all written by the school's seminary faculty, although this is the first one we've seen. It is subtitled *"A Biblical Perspective on Moderation and Abstinence,"* and it is billed on the cover as "A Bob Jones University Seminary Publication," which certainly gives it prestige in the eyes of Christians. The author writes as a concerned Christian who wants to do right and be faithful to Christ and His Word. That is all well and Good, BUT:

The Books Opening

The book opens with a hypothetical question and answer dialogue between a pastor and a potential new member about the church's position on alcohol. When the prospect learns the church's covenant forbids the use of alcohol, even though he really likes the church – "the preaching, the teaching, the fellowship" – he determines "to look somewhere else."

If someone puts his love of booze above his love for a church, we don't think the latter, the church, lost much. And it is certainly easy today to move on and quickly find a church where he can feel comfortable in his sin. The pastor will probably join him in imbibing, and they can enjoy the "shared pleasure" that all booze sellers advertise.

Jaeggli's Introduction

In the introduction, Jaeggli talks about some of the dangers of alcohol and what often happens under the influence of it. It is such strong stuff we would think that any normal person, after reading this section, would say, "I don't need to read the rest of the book and saying or thinking, "I'm going to be an abstainer. Alcoholic Russian roulette is not for me!" Alas, it doesn't work that way, especially if someone is looking for an excuse to 'snort' anyway!

The Warning about Intemperance

However, and this is good, Jaeggli repeatedly warns of "intemperance," which is overindulgence, greed, self-indulgence, hedonism, gluttony, but so does every other promoter of social drinking, sacred or secular – no rational person would argue for *in*temperance. Even the town drunks advocate "moderation" in drinking. The ads of Coors, Miller, Budweiser and even the makers of the 'hard stuff' plead (sincerely or insincerely, you decide) moderation. They know such pious talk about intemperance and moderation will not hurt their sales one bit. So that kind of advertising or speech or writing does not impress us much.

There is no way around it; this book by Dr. Jaeggli is advocating social drinking, "in moderation." However, Dr. Andrew Ivy, a prominent scientist in his lifetime and a vice-president of the University of Illinois, put it like this:

> "Drinking in moderation is not scientific. The only factual or scientific

> guarantee against alcoholism...*is total abstinence.*"

There is no way to discover an alcoholic *until he is an alcoholic*" (emphasis added). As another expressed it, "Neither science nor Seagrams can tell him that." Or as a writer in our local paper put it last Sunday, "...alcohol has become part of relationships – and not everyone is equipped to handle it." In short, many social drinkers end up as alcoholics!

The author tells you where he is headed right off the start:

> "As our survey of the biblical data will show, it is difficult to conclude that biblical wine was unfermented."

21 Hebrew and Greek Words Translated Wine

This is both true and false. Since there are 21 Hebrew and Greek words translated "wine" in the Bible, it depends on which word is used as to what it means. Some reference unfermented, some do not, and some can relate to both. We have a chapter on this in our huge book exposing *Armstrongism* (this cult was very much in favor of "social drinking"; the Armstrongs would have loved Jaeggli's work).

Noah

He starts by noting several Bible characters who got drunk, starting with Noah. We don't know how 'cricket' it is using Noah, however, since he had just entered a new environment after the flood and may not have had any idea what the grape juice he had made was going to do to him – it is the first time wine is mentioned in Scripture. There is not word of him ever getting drunk again (nor having gotten drunk before). He next used Lot, saying, "we know that Lot was a righteous man"; true, but we also know he didn't always live righteously (for example, getting drunk on wine and committing incest with his daughters).

Works That Attack Alcohol

Christian readers who are used to strong attacks on booze by works such as: *The Devil's Juice* by Byron Glaze, The *Deceitfulness of Wine and Strong Drink* by the late Theodore Epp of "Back to the Bible" fame, *The Woe of the Wine Cup* by Sam Morris, *The Double Curse of Booze* by John R. Rice, and even *A Snake in the Bottle* by an author unknown to me, are in for a big shock if they read this book.

In fact, Jaeggli argues that *all* wine has some fermentation since the process commences immediately. (Apparently, even if the one in the wine press stomping on the grapes bends down to drink some of the juice, he would be gulping wine already partly fermented. This, alas, is not scientific at all.)

While he mentions *Bible Wines (or) Laws of Fermentation and Wines of the Ancients*, by William Patton, **a tremendous book,** which he considers "very outdated," if he mentioned what we **consider the best on the subject**, *The Bible and its Wines* by Charles Wesley Ewing, we missed it; Nor did we note him referencing the excellent book by Ernest B. Gordon (son of A. J. Gordon), *Christ, the Apostles and Wine*.

Biblical Context

Jaeggli's look at biblical content and context is very weak. Jaeggli starts in his opening chapter with the Hebrew word *yayin,* one of the major words in any study on this subject (others in the OT are *tirosh, asis* – both of which always mean fresh, unfermented juice – and *shekar* from which our English words sugar and cider are derived).

Ewing calls translating *shekar* as "strong drink" in Deuteronomy `14:26 and other places where it is used,

> "one of the worst translation errors that we have in our English versions."

Hebrew תִּירוֹשׁ = Tirosh

As for *tirosh* (also spelled tiyrosh, tiyrowsh, thirosh, teerosehe, teerosh) no less than the *Jewish Encyclopedia*, surely a significant authority, says it "includes all kinds of sweet juices and must and does not include fermented wine." Note: it ***does not*** include fermented wine! (You would think everyone would acknowledge as usually factual the *Jewish Encyclopedia* in matters Jewish, especially word definitions and would pay close attention to what it said.) Ewing also quotes in support of this definition of tirosh, *The New Schaff-Herzog Encyclopedia of Religious Knowledge;* Heinrich Friedrich Wilhelm Gesenius (the *New International Dictionary of the Christian Church* calls him "the most outstanding Hebraist of his generation") in his *Hebrew German Lexicon*; and others.

Greek Οἶνος = Oinos

In his second chapter, Jaeggli looks at the Greek *oinos* and *gleukos* (the latter used only once in the NT). Unfortunately, most, but not all of the words he uses in his book are generic terms (polysemic terms meaning the coexistence of many possible meanings for a word or phrase) and reference different products in the Word of God, making interpretation more difficult. We were disappointed that he did not *really* examine the main ones, but merely gave an illustration or two of how they were used, which is a *very* insufficient approach for one trying to be scholarly on a *serious* subject, in our judgment. The back cover says he "examines these passages in the light of thorough research," but we strongly disagree with the idea of thorough research (at least in this book). And we think he sadly missed the point of "drunk" and "filled" in Ephesians 5:18, trying to explain why Paul used the two together.

The "Wine" at the Wedding Feast

Jaeggli says the wine that Jesus made at the wedding feast *was alcoholic*! He wants readers to believe that Jesus made between 108 and 162 gallons of intoxicating wine for folks after they had "well drunk" (John 2:10), something that seems incredible to us.

The "Wine" at the Lord's Supper

He argues folks in Christ's day diluted their fermented wine with water, but admits it was still capable of getting them drunk. He insists the 'wine' in the Lord's Supper (although ***never once*** called "wine" in the Word of God) was fermented (meaning rotten, corrupted), but diluted with water. Since the cup represents Christ's blood, it therefore would picture *rotten, corrupted, diluted, watered-down* blood (again something too hard for us to swallow). In fact, I find that impossible to believe, even reprehensible,

Jaeggli does not mention that when Jesus introduced the Lord's Supper to His disciples, since they were observing the Passover – a time when anything fermented was not even allowed in the house to say nothing of on the table – it had to be unfermented.

Luther's Drinking

He mentions Luther's drinking (and the fact that Martin boasted about it), but he doesn't reveal it was beer, the "hard stuff" in the "Bible (strong drink), that the founder of Lutheranism loved to lap up. He also mentions

Calvin, but he had other faults as well – including how he sometimes treated his opposition. He mentions beer as the beverage of choice for Puritans, but if he ever pointed out that was the "strong drink" of Scripture, we missed it.

Billy Sunday

He gives a terrific anti-booze quote by Billy Sunday, but then sums it up,

> "It would be a shame if we, his heirs in the defense and propagation of the gospel, ever fail to issue just as clarion a call against ***the abuse*** of alcohol" (emphasis added).

Wait a minute! *Abuse?* Billy ***never*** crusaded against its ***abuse***; he was in favor of pouring all the slop down the sewer! *(And so are we!)* There never was a bigger enemy of social drinking than Sunday.

Past Argument

Jaeggli talks about past arguments against margarine and smoking, and I am 'agin' them, too. In fact, I never touched the former during all its days of popularity (unless some well-meaning hostess slipped it to me unnoticed while dining at her table). And my position on tobacco is surely well known. But I've never read of "addiction" to margarine or read of anyone becoming a margo (as in wino)! And while tobacco is indeed addictive, I've never read of any husband beating his wife or abusing his kids *because* he smoked a pack. I guess it is easy to compare apples with oranges (something Jaeggli says he doesn't do) if it helps the cause, right?

Medical Views

In his chapter on medical views he quotes enough negative statistics to make one wonder if a person could be considered of "sound mind" if he became a social drinker after reading it, thus taking a chance on becoming an alcoholic. And, remember, *every* social drinker is gambling on not becoming an alcoholic when he takes his *first* drink. It doesn't seem to be a gamble a Christian would be wise to take.

Jaeggli has bought into the brewer's idea that wine is good for the heart, but as we have pointed out repeatedly on these pages, unfermented grape juice offers the same identical benefits (without the wino risk and the damage from alcohol); some scientists say the benefits of the juice are superior to wine.

Holiness

His final chapter on holiness is a good one, but it seems odd to tell someone social drinking is okay, but to remain holy while you are doing it! By the way, the definition of the English word wine *never* meant anything but the sweet juice of the grape until years *after* the KJV was translated. Check any of the dictionaries of that period.

WCTU and Frances Willard

Strangely, in his Conclusion, Jaeggli sounds like Billy Sunday or the local arm of the WCTU (Women's Christian Temperance Union), but we doubt that after 70 pages of "okay on the sauce" it will do much good. Speaking of the WCTU, its early leader Frances Willard noted, "The liquor traffic would destroy the Church if it could, but the Church could destroy the liquor traffic if it would." The reasoning in this volume would *never* destroy it – or even dent it.

Let me give you a final quote from Ewing:

> "Any beverage that contains alcohol contains poison. Fermented wine contains alcohol, a poison, an intoxicant, a hypnotic,

an analgesic, an anesthetic, a potentially habit-forming, craving-producing, addiction-producing drug. To this writer, it is inconceivable that an all wise God, with the best interest of His creatures in mind, would give His sanction to the use of any drink that contains poison, or that is an addiction-producing drug."

Amen to that!

Conclusion

Here is our conclusion: Do you want to become an alcoholic? The only way to be sure you won't is by *not touching* the stuff as a social drinker. No abstainer ever became an alcoholic! "We think this book, while the author may have had good intentions, will do a whole lot more harm than good. We fear some Christians who have never touched the stuff may start, making the author a subject to the curse of Habakkuk 2:15,

> *"Woe unto him that giveth his neighbour drink, that puttest thy bottle to him, and makest him drunken also, that thou mayest look on their nakedness!"*

That makes us sad!

(NOTE: The writer (Dennis Helton) may not necessarily agree 100 percent with all that Dr. Sumner says but I do agree with the gist of his review.)

Comments By Dr. Shelton Smith

The following is by Dr. Shelton Smith of *The Sword of the Lord* newspaper, July 10, 2009:

Recently, (May 2009) a couple of people asked me if I had seen the book *The Christian and Drinking* by Dr. Randy Jaeggli of the Bob Jones University faculty. I had not seen it, but because it was flagged for me by some men that I trust, I ordered a copy.

Published by Bob Jones University Press with a preface of commendation written by Dr. Stephen J. Hankins, the dean of the Bob Jones University Seminary. It is a 72-page paperback book.

Upon receiving it, I read it in one sitting. I must say that I was stunned by what I read. From the pen of a professor at the school founded by Dr. Bob Jones, Sr., and published by that school's publishing arm, there comes this book whose thesis is that the Bible condemns drunkenness and the abuse of alcohol but that it does not condemn drinking alcohol in *moderation.* I could hardly believe I was seeing what I was reading!

Some Quotes

Here are Dr. Jaeggli's quotes on this:

"The Bible makes the consumption of wine wrong for certain people at various times in their lives" (p. 23).

"God intended His people to view alcoholic beverages as a blessing from His hand, just as they appreciated all agricultural products from the land He had given. At a time in history when potable water was not always readily available, alcoholic beverages provided a safe means of hydration – a necessity for life" (p. 27).

"Wine was a blessing only if consumed moderately. The Old Testament contains serious warnings against intemperance. (p. 28).

"Paul does not forbid drinking wine, only drinking to excess (p. 29).

"Because of the potential for causing drunkenness, the New Testament authors mandate moderation in the consumption of wine. It was particularly important for leaders in the church to set a good example in moderation (p. 30).

"In the case of the overseer, Paul states the qualification of moderate use of wine using slightly different terminology. Paul says that the overseer must not be "given to wine" (I Tim. 3:3) (p. 31).

"Just like the Old Testament words for alcoholic beverages, the New Testament words *oinos* and *gleukos* refer to an alcoholic beverage that must be used in moderation. Violation of the principle of moderate use of wine disqualified a person from holding a position of leadership in the church. Older women also needed to be very careful how much they imbibed, because younger women looked to them as examples of Christian virtue" (p. 41).

"It is necessary at this point in our discussion to consider whether the consumption of alcoholic beverages is intrinsically wrong (like the use of illegal

> drugs) or something that a Christian might be able to enjoy without being entrapped by worldliness (like flying his own airplane). Since the Bible does not condemn drinking alcoholic beverages in moderation, could a believer enjoy a glass of his favorite vintage in the privacy of his home and not be ensnared by worldliness? Could he drink wine with dinner at a friend's home? Could he enjoy a pitcher of beer while watching a football game with his friends at the local sports bar? Since "the earth is the Lords', and the fullness thereof" (Ps. 24:1; I Cor. 10:26), why not enjoy a cold brew? These are issues that every Christian needs to settle by wisely applying biblical principles." (pp. 68, 69).

After Reading the Book

After reading the book and carefully pondering the issue it raises, I placed a phone call to Dr. Jaeggli (pronounced yea-glee). Although I do not know him, I was glad to talk with him for approximately twenty minutes. Our conversation was open and direct about the issue but was gracious throughout.

In his defense, let me be clear that Dr. Jaeggli says in the book that he himself does not drink and more than once he advises against drinking. He said to me,

> "I am against drinking. It is unwise for anyone to do it."

He was very adamant that he does not support drinking alcohol at all.

Cultural Considerations

But the thrust of the entire book is that the Bible does not condemn the drinking of alcohol. It does, he says, condemn drunkenness but not drinking in moderation.

It is true that the Bible does not condemn the moderate consumption of alcoholic beverages within an ancient cultural setting that mandated their use for safe hydration as a necessary part of life. But drinking today is not comparable to biblical times.

Modern drinks are far more intoxicating. We have plenty of nonalcoholic options for safe hydration. We ought to be growing in holiness and not cozying up to the world system. Let's be careful to set the biblical standard correctly for the generation that follows us, "Whether therefore ye eat, or drink or whatsoever ye do, do all to the glory of God" (I Cor. 10:31).

Temperance Movement

In our conversation, Dr. Jaeggli said,

> "For 1,900 years godly people did not think there was anything wrong with drinking in moderation. It was only when the temperance movement came on the scene in the early 1800's that total abstinence became a practice."

He does not offer any documentation for this. It is, I believe, an incorrect assumption that lacks historical credibility.

In an effort to clarify his position, he also said to me, "Modern drinking is not the same as first century drinking."

Alcoholic drinks today are much stronger because the ancient people watered them down, according to Dr.

Jaeggli. Herein again I believe there is a presumption of fact which cannot be supported.

BOB JONES UNIVERSITY POSITION ON ALCOHOL CONSUMPTION

The Bob Jones University website has a three-paragraph statement entitled: "The Position of Bob Jones University and Seminary Regarding a Christian's Consumption of Alcohol." The definitive part of that statement says:

> "As a Christian fundamentalist educational institution, Bob Jones University has taken a consistent stand for complete abstinence from the use of alcohol since our inception in 1927. Bob Jones University does not believe the Scripture condones the beverage use of alcohol by Bible-believing Christians. We will not retain a faculty or staff member or a student who uses alcohol or promotes its use.
>
> "Bob Jones University believes that the Christian is called to a life of growing conformity to the image of Christ and that the beverage use of alcohol hinders this conformity and growth in personal holiness. It is the University's position that total abstinence is crucial to the believer's unhindered and unobscured testimony – in the home, among fellow believes in the church, in the workplace and in society at large."

Contradictory Advice

So the University is strong on its "no drinking" position. Dr. Jaeggli, the author of the book, also says "no drinking" is his position and practice.

However, in the preface of the book (p. vii), Dr. Hawkins, the Dean of the seminary, says that this book is a part of a series designed

> "...to provide help in finding this right, discerning balance in spiritual life...."

We simply cannot reconcile stated assurances with the purposeful publication of this book. It does not seem consistent to us to say "the Bible does not condemn it" but we do! There is an inconsistency there that I believe is going to trip up a lot of people.

I also phoned Dr. Stephen Jones, the president of Bob Jones University, but at press time he had not returned my call.

Sword Editorial Opinion of Dr. Jaeggli's Book

While I do not question Dr. Jaeggli's sincerity, I do have major problems with his position on this and with the wisdom of publishing such a treatise as this. He is, I'm convinced, a sincere Christian man, but I believe he is sincerely wrong on this.

He is an academic, and he has approached this from what he believes to be a scholarly angle. There are, however, some serious issues with his approach.

Dr. Jaeggli makes much of his point that the unsafe drinking water in that time necessitated the drinking of wine to keep oneself properly hydrated. We believe that this idea lacks credibility for several reasons.

No Credibility for Wine for Hydration

First, there are wells all over the pages of the Bible. Much ado is made about the wells. They were there and they were in use.

Second, if they were using wine for hydrating the body, everybody would have been drunk all the time.

Third, alcohol consumption contributes to dehydration (not hydration) of the body. If alcohol is the sole source of hydration, the health issues are quick to surface. When going to a desert area (such as the Middle East) for extended periods, it is a basic rule of thumb that alcohol consumption is to be restricted.

So very candidly, the "no safe water" reasoning for drinking alcoholic wine just doesn't "hold water" at all (as we say). It is a very old argument that is typically employed by weak Christians looking for a way to justify their desire to drink alcohol. It is not a new idea at all, and we are frankly surprised that Dr. Jaeggli would make it a part or his argument.

Hebrew and Greek Words Use Not Supported

He also utilizes the Hebrew (Old Testament) words and the Greek (New Testament) words to undergird his position. There are, however, other definitive studies done on these same words that do not support Dr. Jaeggli's position.

Care of the highest order must be used when consulting Hebrew and Greek texts and lexicons to avoid getting the wrong slant on word meanings. We believe his linguistic analysis is subject to other interpretations which would place his entire thesis in dispute.

Consequently, we do not recommend Dr. Jaeggli's book for any purpose! It is, we believe, a dangerous book that will cause many to stumble. We think that Bob Jones University Press would be well advised to rethink this and cease the publication and distribution of the book

Drunkenness But Not Drinking?

Although it is without dispute that the book is totally devoted to its thesis, namely that the Bible condemns drunkenness but not drinking, the author does make some attempt to show the risk of abuse if alcohol is permitted.

He does not, however, have even one single quote by the great men of God who have thundered so loudly about the use of alcohol. His warnings about using alcohol today are limited to a few paragraphs. Approximately 70 of the 72 pages are given over to making the case that the Bible condemns drunkenness but not drinking.

Many of our churches now have ministries like "Reformers Unanimous" that reach those with alcohol problems. I can't imagine that this book would be anything but trouble in such ministries.

In part two of this article (in the July 24 issue of the SWORD OF THE LORD), we will make our case on what we believe about the Christian's use of alcohol (we are against it, and we believe the Bible condemns it).

The following is by an oped writer to The Times Examiner newspaper (copied from *The Times Examiner* newspaper of Greenville, SC, August 12, 2009, p. 6.)

> "Dear Editor,
>
> Christians should lodge a strong protest and rebuttal against the book "The Christian And Drinking" by Dr. Randy Jaeggli who is on the Bob Jones University faculty.
>
> It defies all logic and common sense that a Christian professor would take the time, and put forth the effort to write a book that is contrary to the Word of God, and that is not godly and beneficial instruction to believers.
>
> In his book he contends that the Bible does not condemn drinking in moderation by Christians. However, the

admonition is clear in Proverbs 23:20, 31 not to even be among winebibbers, and also not to even look upon the wine when it is fermented.

No matter what Dr. Jaeggli's academic credentials may be, he is not the authority on the drinking of alcohol; the Word of God is, and it says in Proverbs 20:1

> *"Wine is a mocker, strong drink is raging and whosoever is deceived thereby is not wise."*

On this thought it is appropriate to quote Romans 3:4,

> "Let God be true, but every man a liar."

The statistics are that one out of every nine people who take the first drink of alcohol becomes an alcoholic. Why would any rational thinking Christian make the assertion that God condones a behavior that destroys lives?

We Christians also owe it to our children and grandchildren to take a responsible stand against the consumption of booze and set the record straight.

Eddie Cox – Greer, SC

THE FOLLOWING POSITION IS BY DENNIS HELTON

In 1975, several students of BJU told this writer of a professor's teaching at BJU (not Dr. Jaeggli) who taught that Jesus made fermented wine at the marriage supper of Cana (name withheld because of the lack of written documentation). The claim of this professor's teaching (that Christ made fermented wine in John chapter 2) began to come to this writer as early as 1974. Even the chaplain (Captain in the Army Reserve) at Clemson, SC where this writer was serving a one year Army Reserve commitment, claimed to be a former student of this same professor and confirmed this story about the Professor's teaching. The Army captain was challenged when he requested that a soldier of the Army supply room obtain fermented wine for an open Communion at the Clemson Army Reserve Center. This writer was stationed there for a one-year enlistment as an E-5 reservist radio mechanic and was present to observe this occasion personally. Two other BJU students shared rides with this writer from Greenville, SC to the Clemson Army Reserve Center.

Bible students are very impressionable and tend to erroneously consider their college professors to be the final authority on Bible interpretation (exegesis).

Reasons Against the Consumption of Fermented Wine:

Fermentation (of any kind) **typifies** death, decay and rot. (The physical resultant of death is carbonic acid, water, carbon dioxide gas, and other waste products).

In the New Testament, leaven [a producer (cause) of fermentation] is a type of evil, false doctrine, and malice. Leaven (ferment) was not permitted to be in the Jew's household during the Passover. Would Jesus use "fermented" grape juice to symbolize His shed blood? Absolutely not! Forget about your knowledge of Hebrew and Greek, the Holy Spirit leads and guides us into all truth. The Bible sheds a lot of light upon the anemic hermeneutics (principles of interpretation) of educated and uneducated men.

Would Jesus have made fermented wine knowing that the only way a sinner could become a drunkard was to take his first drink.

Also, consider that some drinkers of alcoholic drinks have a body metabolism that render them far more prone to addiction to drugs and alcohol than others.

The Bible expressly forbids any drunkard from inheriting the kingdom of God. **I Corinthians 6:10:**

> *Nor thieves, nor covetous, **nor drunkards**, nor revilers, nor extortioners, shall inherit the kingdom of God.*

Would Jesus have made fermented wine (at the marriage supper of Cana) knowing that it would be in contradiction to many other Scriptures (Proverbs 20:1; 23:20, 21, 29-33; Habakkuk 2:15; I Corinthians 6:10). The Scriptures do not contradict one another.

Although a saved person is capable of committing adultery, telling lies, stealing, or even consuming fermented wine, that does justify the acts nor give any credibility to sin.

The Production of Alcohol

Fermented wine is an art of man. Fermented wine to any significant amount does not occur in nature (a few grapes lying in a favorable climate for a short while and producing a tinge of alcohol does not constitute alcoholic production). In order for alcoholic fermentation to occur, at least three things must be constant (1) temperature, (2) concentration, and (3) leaven (leaven = yeast; ferment; gleukos). If these elements that are essential to fermentation are not closely adhered to, we may obtain vinegar (acetic acid) or non-alcoholic drink.

The Leading of the Holy Spirit or Education

In the passage of the Lord's Supper, even the Greek word **οἶνος** (used for both fermented and unfermented wine) is glaringly absent (note; unfermented grape juice was commonly called wine in the wine in the Bible). So how do the "so-called" scholars translate *cup* and *fruit of the vine* as alcoholic beverage? The writer is so thankful that education is not the primary ingredient for properly interpreting Scriptures, else only professors of Hebrew and Greek could have the potential to understand God's Word.

This writer would fear to drink "this cup" unworthily (such as symbolizing Christ's blood with a leavened beverage) lest he be guilty of the blood of the Lord, and be judged of Him and even die a premature death ("a sin unto death" – I John 5:16; Romans 6:16).

I Corinthians 11:29-30:

*For he that eateth and drinketh unworthily, eateth and drinketh **damnation** to himself, not discerning the Lord's body. For this cause many are weak and sickly among you, and many **sleep**.*

Dr. Jaeggli stated that he does not condone drinking alcoholic wine but the Bible allows it. So, Dr. Jaeggli does not allow drinking alcoholic wine but the Bible does! Does Dr. Jaeggli think that his personal concept of abstaining from drinking alcoholic wine is wiser than God's standard of holiness? Of course, a believer can sin; a believer can drink wine; a believer can curse; a believer can lie; a believer can commit sins of disobedience (not a continual lifestyle of sin) and even commit a "sin unto death, but these things have nothing to do with the actual salvation experience of being "born again" (John 3:3-7). If a sinning believer does not confess and forsake his sin, he is likely to die a premature death (I John 5:16; Romans 6:16; Hebrews 12:6-8; I Corinthians 11:29-32). It is this writer's opinion that it is very dangerous to tread carelessly upon the symbol of Christ's blood which is symbolized by "unfermented" wine. The sinless blood of Jesus Christ is holy ground and trampling upon it is much worse than committing common sin.

It appears that Dr. Jaeggli thinks drinking fermented wine in moderation is permissible. Is lying, cheating, idolatry, fornicating, etc. "in moderation" also acceptable (I Corinthians 6:9-19)? All of these sins are explicitly condemned in Scriptures.

Knowing the great potential harm that such a book as Dr. Jaeggli's could do to babes in Christ, carnal believers, former alcoholics, and the unsaved, is it wise to use the energy and time to publish such a book? You might as well endorse a host of other ungodly acts, "in moderation" of course (satire).

Please refer to other papers on the subject of alcoholic beverages by the author (Dennis Helton). The writer has much more to say concerning wine in the Bible but enough has already been said to touch the heart of the sincere believer. Here are some comments by other famous authors:

COMMENTS BY OTHER FAMOUS AUTHORS

-Shakespeare: "Alcohol is a poison men take into the mouth to steal away the brain."

-Gladstone: Strong drink is "more destructive than war, pestilence and famine."

-Sir Wilfred Lawson: "The devil in solution."

-Abraham Lincoln: "A cancer in human society, eating out its vitals and threatening its destruction."

-Robert Hall: "Distilled damnation."

-Lord Chesterfield: "An artist in human slaughter."

-Ruskin: "The most criminal and artistic method of assassination ever invented by the bravos of any age or nation."

-General Pershing: "Drunkenness has killed more men than of history's wars."

-Robert E. Lee: "My experience through life has convinced me that abstinence from spirituous liquors is the best safeguard to morals and health."

-President Taft: "He who drinks is deliberately disqualifying himself for administration."

PRESERVING UNFERMENTED WINE IN BIBLE TIMES

by

Pastor David R. Brumbelow
P. O. Box 300, Lake Jackson, TX 77566

A Christian speaks against alcohol and explains how the biblical words for wine were used to refer to nonalcoholic, as well as alcoholic wine. A scholar replies, "But it was impossible to keep wine from fermenting in the ancient world. No one could do this until Louis Pasteur and Welch's in the late 1800s."

He adds for good measure, "The Passover wine had to be fermented because it was in the Spring, long after the Fall grape harvest." That seems an unanswerable argument.

Those who use this argument think they are rightly interpreting Scripture. Instead, they are taking their own ignorance and projecting it onto the Bible and the ancient world. To argue that the ancients could not preserve un-intoxicating wine is wrong factually, scientifically, and historically. Actually, fermented wine was more difficult to make and preserve, than unfermented wine.

Unfermented wine could easily be preserved without electricity, refrigeration, or pasteurization. Following are several examples.

Reduce Its Consistency

One way is to boil fresh expressed wine down to about a third or fifth of its consistency. This thick, strong wine or syrup would keep without fermentation. When ready to drink, it would just be mixed with water. This was also done with cider and other fruit.

Patrick E. McGovern is a pro-drinking secular authority on ancient and modern wine. He said,

> "Concentrating grape juice down by heating is still used to make the popular shireh of modern Iran and was known to the ancient peoples of Mesopotamia as well as the Greeks and Romans. It enables fruit to be preserved, and, diluted with water, it produces a refreshing, nonalcoholic beverage." (Ancient Wine: The Search For The Origins Of Viniculture by Patrick E. McGovern, Princeton University Press, Princeton, New Jersey, 2003).

Tischendorf wrote of a visit to Coptic monasteries in Egypt in 1845,

> "Instead of wine they use a thick juice of the grape, which I at first mistook for oil."

Aristotle said the wine of Arcadia was so thick it was necessary to scrape it from the wineskins and dissolve it in water (Patton, Bible Wines, this book, as well as others in English and Spanish are available at:
www.theoldpathspublications.com).

Length of the Grape Harvest

The grape harvest lasted six months. This was done by planting different varieties of grapes, and planting them in different microclimates. Ancient writers testified of the vast number of varieties of grapes; some said they were innumerable. Grape vines and cuttings were transported throughout the Roman world.

Israel was at the crossroads of the world. Agriculture was their life. Some vines bear an early harvest, some midseason, some late. The first grapes can be picked as early as July, the latest in December. Some vines ripen all their grapes at once; others over a long period of time. Some grapes bore two crops a year. Grapes right off the vine were available for half the year.

It was a common practice to squeeze a bunch of grapes by hand directly into a cup and drink that fresh, sweet (fermentation takes away the sweetness) unfermented wine. "Then Pharaoh's cup was in my hand; and I took the grapes and pressed them into Pharaoh's cup, and placed the cup in Pharaoh's hand" (Genesis 40:11). Historian Josephus refers to this. Pharaoh apparently preferred his wine fresh and unfermented.

A stone relief found in the Roman city of Pompeii pictures the god of wine (in sore need of a loincloth), squeezing grapes by hand into a cup (Patton, Bible Wines). Early church writings referred to pressing grapes into a cup for the Lord's Supper.

Grapes Preserved Fresh

Grapes could be preserved fresh for months. Some will protest their grapes don't keep long. Let me explain. Any old-time gardener will tell you some fruits and vegetables are "good keepers," others are not. A good keeper, at room temperature, can remain fresh for months. This was especially well-known in ancient times when such knowledge could mean the difference between going hungry or not, or even prevent starvation.

Characteristics of good "keeping" grapes include a tough skin and adhering well to the cluster. The cluster would be cut from the vine. Any bad grapes would be clipped, not pulled, from the cluster. Pulling a grape leaves a "brush" that can start a molding, decaying process. Grape clusters were loosely packed in straw, cotton, bran, or hung from the ceiling. Periodically they would be inspected, and any bad grapes clipped off.

The right varieties of grapes stored in this way would last fresh for months. Leon C. Field, Methodist scholar, said, in 1883, "Niebuhr says that, 'the Arabs preserve grapes by hanging them up in their cellars, and eat them almost through the whole year.' Dr. Kerr says, 'A friend of mine now in Britain not long since unpacked grapes he had received eleven months previously from the continent, finding them fresh and good.'"

Also, "Bernier says grapes were sent from Persia to India, wrapped in cotton, two hundred years ago, and sold there throughout the year."

An early 1800s recipe book, called "receipts" back then, gives directions that would preserve grapes fresh for 12 months. These grapes could be pressed into a cup at any time of the year.

Made from Dried Grapes

Wine was also made from dried grapes or raisins. Drying is one of the oldest methods of preserving food. Raisins were rehydrated by soaking or boiling and pressed into wine.

The Talmud (ancient Jewish writings) refers to raisin wine. Polybius (Greek historian c. 100 BC) spoke of un-intoxicating raisin wine. A medieval Arabian writer refers to raisin wine for the Lord's Supper. Modern day Jews refer to raisin wine.

Sealing "Must"

Seal "must" in amphora (wine container). Roman writer Cato (c. 170 BC) said, "If you would keep must [new unfermented wine] for a year, pour it into an amphora and seal the cork with pitch. Immerse the amphora in cold water for thirty days. Then remove it and the must will be preserved for one year" (De Agri Cultura).

Additionally, olive oil and resin were used to make containers and contents airtight. Filtering was claimed to break the strength of wine. Chemical additives were used. Fermented wine could be boiled to remove the alcohol.

The above methods were widely practiced and provided unfermented wine throughout the year. So, don't let anyone tell you, scholar or otherwise, that in Bible times they had no choice but to drink fermented wine.

Further Study

For further study: Alcohol Today, Peter Lumpkins; The Bible and its Wines, Charles Wesley Ewing; Bible Wines, William Patton; Fights I Didn't Start, And Some I Did, R. L. Sumner; Communion Wine, William M. Thayer; Libertinism: A Baptist and His Booze, Jerry Vines; Oinos, Leon C. Field. (see the bookstore for further help:
www.theoldpathspublications.com

ABOUT THE AUTHOR

The writer was born in Greenville, SC in 1934 and was a lifetime resident except for two years in the US Army (Fort Jackson, S.C. and Fort Carson, Colorado) and two years residence in Florida.

After separation (honorably) from the US Army, the writer returned to Greenville, SC and married at age 27 to Christine Moore, an old acquaintance from an adjacent neighborhood. The Lord blessed us with six daughters, Debbie, Donna, Dale, Denise, Deree, and Dena.

A short time after marriage, the writer was convicted of his lost condition as a sinner and after a miserable time under conviction the writer confessed his sin and lost condition to God and was saved.

The writer was 40 years of age when he began attending college (3 years, no diploma).

The writer retired as a chemical technologist from Morton International Chemical Company in 1996. Before retirement, the writer had the urge to write on Bible subjects and wished that he had more time to study. Upon retirement, the writer bought a computer and became a novice writer.

The writer now resides in Easley, S.C.

D. Helton has written several documents and books, as well as the books or booklets: "Jesus is God," "Evolution, Another False Religion of Humanism," "Cremation: Christian or Pagan," "Is The Gap Theory Credible?" "Does Water Baptism Save," "Can a Saved Person Become Unsaved," and several others, available here:

http://www.theoldpathspublications.com/Pages/Authors/Helton.htm#God

www.ingramcontent.com/pod-product-compliance
Lightning Source LLC
LaVergne TN
LVHW020312110826
845148LV00017BA/2642

* 9 7 8 1 7 3 6 5 3 4 4 0 3 *